"God, Thank You for the Morning"

Sister Patricia A. Cruise, S.C.

Covenant House

DEDICATED
To all the children
who will sleep on America's streets tonight —
scared, cold, hungry,
and desperate to find someone who cares.

Table of Contents

Introduction 5

"They tracked me down
and set me on fire." 11

He's part of our family now... 15

"I didn't count how many times
he raped me..." 19

"When your mother is threatening to
kill you, you just run." 23

"I was born into a gang..." 27

They come to us with numb hearts... 31

"It's my mother's ashes..." 37

"She's a cutter..." 41

Learning to fly... 47

Covenant House is their last hope... 51

"Adam was five when his father
sold him for use as a sex toy…"   57

"They made me keep the
 handcuffs on…"   61

"He's going to kill me…"   65

"Reality hit me … I was 15
and a runaway…"   73

"Sometimes I hope the next
bullet has my name on it…"   79

 "Footprints"   85

"Your outreach workers
saved my life that night…"   89

The American Family   93

Family Survival Guide   94

Introduction

The anonymous handwritten note was left on the altar in our chapel.

"Dear God, I want to thank you for helping me through another day. Thank you for the morning. It gets harder and harder. Please watch my back, God. And if anything should happen to me, please take my soul."

Every night, on the streets of the richest country in the world, there is a nameless, faceless army of forgotten children fighting to survive. Eating food out of dumpsters. Sleeping in alleyways. Trying to survive in a world where no one loves them.

And praying to God to watch their backs so they can live to see the next morning.

My name is Sister Patricia Cruise, and I am the President of Covenant House, the largest system of emergency shelters – and the most important source of second chances – for homeless children in America. We serve almost 2,000 children a night – young people from all walks of life and from all parts of the country.

There is a perception that if a child runs away, he or she is a bad kid – not true. The overwhelming majority of children don't run away from a good, loving environment – and if they do, we can usually get them back home within a day or two.

The children on our streets and in our Covenant House shelters are not on a teen-age lark. They come to us with tragic stories of sexual abuse, physical assault and emotional violation by parents, stepparents, or other adults in their lives. They tell us about what happened to them when they escaped home and ended up on the streets... stories that are frightening enough to make me wonder how they ever found the strength and courage to survive among the pimps, drug dealers, gang members, and other street predators ready to use them, exploit them, and throw them away.

Our mission at Covenant House is to reach these children before they disappear into the streets, before they become victims of the violent street war being shamefully fought every night in cities all across this country. I believe God has called us to protect his most forgotten children, and I pray you join me in the fight.

This book is my attempt to tell the stories of some of our children. They are not pretty stories, but if you read them, you will meet some amazing young people. Like Robbie, who was beaten and set on fire by a gang, but found the courage to pull himself through a painful recovery and credits God with saving his life. Or Jane, who came to us on Christmas Eve and begged to stay, saying Covenant House was the closest thing she had to a family.

When you read these stories, you will meet kids who have lived through a hell that you and I can barely imagine ... and yet they still believe in heaven. They still find the incredible inner strength, the faith, and the courage to fight on.

This year, Covenant House will care for 80,000 homeless and runaway children in cities all across America – in New York, Anchorage, Atlanta, Atlantic City, Detroit, Fort Lauderdale, Houston, Los Angeles, Newark, New Orleans, Oakland, Orlando, Philadelphia, St. Louis and

Washington, D.C. As you read this, we are also saving children in shelters throughout Central America, as well as in Toronto, Vancouver and Mexico City. And for those who don't find their way to our doors, we also run a 24-hour hotline, the Covenant House Nineline (1-800-999-9999) which last year received over 50,000 calls from young people in crisis.

The fact is that Covenant House spends more to help homeless children than the federal government. We give the children a place to stay and warm food and clothes. We make sure they get medical care if they need it. We help them heal and start over.

When I took my vow to serve God and the Sisters of Charity 25 years ago, I never imagined writing a book about America's street children. But I believe God has led me here. These children are my family now, and I hope this book will be an effective way to make more people aware that there are good children selling themselves and dying on our streets. I pray that this book will prevent children from running away and will involve more people — people like you — in being part of the solutions to the grave problems our children face.

It is time for all of us to build a world safe for all our children.

Sister Patricia A. Cruise, S.C.
President
Covenant House

Run Away

Scared and cold,
First night on the streets
Your body hurts
From your head to your feet

You miss school,
Not the work – it's the friends
Thinking what you'll say
When they ask where you've been

Gotta dollar fifty,
Every penny gotta spend
Make a wrong move … Boom,
Your life comes to an end.

Daniel, 16, street kid

Dear God, sometimes I can hear
You but I can't understand your words.
Please help me understand so
I may do well. Just think of me as
an angel in training. Yours truly...

Written by a Covenant House
resident in our chapel

God, please stop the pain.

Anonymous note left in our chapel

Chapter 1

"They tracked me down and set me on fire."

I apologize for the graphic nature of this letter, but every word of Robbie's story is true. The fact he is still alive is a miracle, plain and simple.

"I was staying at a friend's house, and these guys broke in and shot him dead right in front of me, Sister," Robbie said. "There were four of them. I started running, but they were too fast. They tackled me and knocked me out. I don't know why they didn't just shoot me, too. Anyway, the next thing I knew, I was waking up smelling burning flesh. They set me on fire.

"To this day, I don't know how I dragged myself to the side of the road," Robbie said. "But I did. Then I passed out and the next thing I remember is being in the hospital. I can't describe how much I hurt.

"When they finally let me out of the hospital, I just started walking. That's when it hit me. There was no one in the world I could turn to. It was a terrible feeling. After a long time, I stopped at a bus bench and said to myself, now what?

"There were these three guys there — one of them must have seen how lost I looked and said, 'Hey, you're ok, you have a place to stay. We're staying at

Covenant House.' I told him I only had $6 to my name, and he said, that's enough to ride the next bus with us. That's how I learned about Covenant House."

"I'm so glad you found us," I told Robbie. "If you don't mind me asking, how did you end up on the street?"

"Well… I was in a gang, Sister," he said, and for the first time his eyes left mine and dropped to the floor. "My mom and dad split when I was a kid. My dad remarried but moved away with his new wife, and I got put in group homes. Those were terrible, I ran from every one of them, and finally hooked up with some other kids on the street."

Surveys indicate there are 750,000 teen and young adult gang members. Most, like Robbie, are alone, searching for any kind of human connection. The fact that thousands of homeless children feel turning to a gang is their only option illustrates how much work we all need to do together to take better care of our children.

"Didn't take long to figure out life on the street with a gang wasn't the answer," Robbie said. "But the thing about a gang, Sister, is once you want out, it ain't easy. I mean, you can't exactly go, 'I quit,' and they go, 'Fine, no problem.' When I tried to get out, that's when they tracked me down, killed my friend, and set me on fire.

"But you know, Sister, while I was recovering from skin grafts in the hospital, I had a lot of time to think. I mean, it wasn't like I had any visitors or anything. I decided right then and there that God must want me alive for a reason. Once I was able, I even started writing some stuff down about my life, about some of the things that have happened to me."

"I would love to hear some of what you wrote," I told Robbie. After hesitating for a few moments, he quietly recited from memory the most haunting, inspirational piece of street poetry I've ever heard:

> *Been down, been shot, been burned*
> *After all, I have learned*
>
> *To seek and find a way*
> *To be safe for this day*
>
> *Somehow I got the nod*
> *To reach out to my God*

Can you see now why I need to do all I can to keep Robbie safe at Covenant House and help him build a life away from the streets, from the gangs that almost killed him?

"Thank you God, for giving me the strength to walk away from drugs. And please, give me the strength to stay off them."

Tim, 15

Chapter 2

"He's part of our family, now."

"Are you a millionaire, Sister Tricia?" 16-year-old Billy asked.

The question came at dinner, my favorite time at Covenant House, a time when most of the kids are in one place and I get to really talk to them about what's going on in their lives. (Maybe it's the same with your family?)

It is also the best time for the kids to ask me questions and some of them — like this one from Billy — are beauties.

I laughed and told him I'm no millionaire, that being a nun means having very little money.

"Then how do you run this place?" he said, waving his fork in the air over his head, as if he needed to draw my attention to the dozens of hungry teenagers surrounding us in our cafeteria on this typically busy night at Covenant House. "How do you get the money?"

I told him I asked people for it.

"What do you say?" he shot back, and I'm sure he now thought I was about to divulge the secret to lifelong financial happiness.

I said to him, well, if you had money and I asked you for some of it to help a lot of really good kids who had no place to stay, wouldn't you give it?

And he said yes. And he got real quiet and put down his fork. And then he started to cry.

Maybe it was because Billy was genuinely touched when it hit him that some people really cared about him. Or maybe it was because it was the first time in a long time someone called him *good*.

Billy has spent all 16 years of his life thinking he is no good. Why else would his father leave right after he was born? Why else would his overwhelmed single mother tell him he was on his own, that she just couldn't care for him anymore when he turned 15. Why else would people on the street use and abuse him? It had to be all his fault, didn't it?

Can you imagine going through life knowing your Dad rejected you when you were a cute little baby? Can you imagine what it must have been like for a 15-year-old boy – a child – to have your Mom say, "You've got to leave. I won't take care of you anymore?"

And then can you imagine what Billy went through as a defenseless, all-alone 15-year-old on the streets, cold, hungry and alone? The pain and rejection Billy is carrying around with him is a burden no child should ever have to bear.

Do you remember what it was like when you were a teenager and you were going through a tough time and one of your parents looked you in the eye and said, "I think you're a great kid. I love you." It was the greatest feeling in the world, wasn't it? It is a feeling Billy has never known.

I believe God sent us Billy, and I believe God sent us friends like you to put food in his stomach and a roof over his head. But more than that, I think God put us together – you and me, at this special place called Covenant House – so we can look a kid like Billy in the eye and let him know that despite how badly he feels right now, despite the rejection and disappointment he has suffered his whole life, he belongs.

He is a part of God's family. And part of our family.

As I humbly ask you to renew your support for our mission together, I want you to know that I firmly believe Covenant House is not about money, or charity.

We need those things, of course. I have to keep asking for your donations, your charity for our kids. We couldn't keep the doors open without your help. That's a simple fact.

But more than the food, clothing, and shelter that we provide, what Covenant House means is a promise – a Covenant of acceptance. I believe with all my heart that communicating this acceptance to kids like Billy is what God wants us to do most of all. If Covenant House could do only one thing, this should be it.

Dear God,

*I just want someone to love me,
someone to talk to when I need to talk.
Someone to cry on when I need to cry.
Most of all someone to love me and
walk as far as they wish through my life.
Amen.*

Chapter 3

"I didn't count how many times he raped me, and I won't tell you the terrible things he did to me when he kept me locked in that filthy bathroom.

"Sister, I had been walking all night, like I had for six days because I was afraid to fall asleep on the street. It was almost dawn, and this car stopped next to me. A guy jumped out, pushed me into the back seat and sped away."

It happened <u>that</u> fast – another child snatched.

"I begged him, I said, 'Please, Mister, you don't want to take me. People will be looking for me, and you'll get in trouble.' Of course, that was a lie. My parents threw me out. No one would know I was gone. I was, like, totally alone."

If you had been sitting with me next to Kayla as she told me her story... and seen her eyes brimming with tears... it would have torn your heart out.

Kayla was able to escape from that windowless bathroom one night when the man who abducted her accidentally left the door unlocked. We found her on the street, her clothing ripped and filthy.

I thank God that you care about abandoned children like Kayla. If we didn't have your support, I don't know what would have happened to her.

With your help, we were able to bring Kayla here to our shelter. We provided her with her first decent meal in days, a clean set of clothes and the medical care she desperately needed.

Kayla's story is shocking. <u>But what's even more shocking is that she never showed up on an AMBER Alert</u>.

You've probably heard of AMBER Alerts. They've been in the news a lot lately because of kidnappings in California and Florida. When a distraught parent reports an abducted child, AMBER Alerts are posted on highways and broadcast on television and radio in hopes of rescuing them.

But all abducted children who show up on AMBER Alerts have <u>one</u> thing in common – a parent who loves them and wants them back.

That's why you and I never saw Kayla's sweet young face on TV. For unwanted children, there are no AMBER Alerts...because nobody reported them missing.

Kids who have been abandoned by their parents – or have run away from abusive homes – don't have any family members looking for them, trying desperately to get them back. They have no one to turn to for help.

<u>And there are sexual predators who know that</u>.

There are actually child molesters out there who prowl the streets, looking for homeless children.

The danger these boys and girls face is so great that we don't wait for them to come to us. We go to them. We go to teen hangouts as well as out-of-the-way tenements and seedy hotels.

Sometimes we'll spend eight hours a day driving from street to street, stopping and talking to kids and handing out bag lunches.

We let them know they are always welcome at Covenant House – that our doors are always open. We tell them about our Nineline (1-800-999-9999), our hotline number which they can call for help, any time of day or night.

We absolutely *must* get to these children first – before the child molesters do.

As horrible as Kayla's story is, I have to tell you – she's one of the lucky ones. A lot of kids who are abducted the way she was end up dead.

That's why I'm so determined to provide food and shelter to abused, unloved kids. I've made a covenant to never, ever, turn away a child in need.

So far, I've been able to keep my promise of hope to these children – thanks to you. Your generosity lets us offer counseling, support and safety to a child whose innocence has been brutally ripped away.

Can you imagine what Kayla felt, alone in that filthy bathroom?

<u>Crying from fear and pain</u>... <u>terrified of what her abductor would do to her when he came back</u>... <u>and thinking that nobody cared whether she lived or died</u>?

No child should ever have to feel so horribly alone.

That's why I pray you will help us protect her and all the other homeless kids living on the streets.

"Sister," Kayla told me through her tears, "I used to pray in church, but I was just saying the words. When I was in that horrible place with that awful man, I talked to God. He guided me through the darkest, most painful times."

I wish no child ever had to go through the pain and fear that Kayla did. I pray that someday there will be a way to include runaway and abandoned children like her in the AMBER Alert system.

But until that day comes, I need your help to protect these vulnerable kids from becoming the next victim.

Please – help me care for these unwanted boys and girls who have no family to love or care for them.

Your gift, of whatever amount you can share, will help us offer food, clean clothes, shelter – and above all, safety – to children who have been hurt in sickening ways.

Your gift will show a child like Kayla that you do care what happens to her.

For kids who have experienced some of the worst brutality you can imagine, these simple things can help them begin to put the pieces of their shattered lives back together.

Chapter 4

"When your mother is high as a kite and threatening to kill you, you just run..."

I never feared winter until I became President of Covenant House.

Now I dread it. I keep seeing these images in my mind of homeless kids freezing on the streets, and I've been praying to God with an urgency I haven't felt in a long, long time.

Staff on our outreach vans and at the front doors of our shelters are trained to know the symptoms of frostbite and hypothermia, because we know we'll see hundreds of dangerously cold, sick kids this winter. All the common sense measures to avoid frostbite — dressing in layers, changing out of wet clothes, avoiding long stretches of exposure to the cold — are all options not available to a child on the street.

That is why this **BED & BLANKET DRIVE** is the most important appeal I will send to you this year. Before the cold weather sets in, I need to ask you to make a contribution to make sure we can get through the winter and give each child who comes to us a safe place to sleep and good food to eat.

I'll also need to be able to fill our outreach vans with winter coats and warm blankets every night as we try to save the lives of the kids who don't find their way to our front door.

I don't know how our kids think they're going to survive on the streets in winter. Many kids come to us with barely enough clothing for a chilly October day, never mind a numbing December or January snow-storm.

I guess the answer is simple – these kids aren't thinking that far ahead. They don't have the luxury to think. You don't think about packing a hat and gloves when your father is threatening to beat you again. Or when your stepfather is drunk and wants sex again. Or when your mother is high as a kite and is threatening to kill you. You just run.

I know your heart aches for these kids as much as mine does. The pain they endure – the indignity of being scared and alone and desperate and so cold you can barely think straight, let alone feel good about yourself – is way too much for any child to bear.

But there is one silver lining in these dark clouds of winter. Winter drives homeless children to our shelters. *As awful as it sounds, the desperation of the cold and the overwhelming need to get warm often pushes kids past the barriers – the fear, the pride, the embarrassment, the anger – and forces them to seek the help they so desperately need.*

And so we must be ready. We must give these kids warm, safe beds to sleep in. And if together we can do that one simple thing, God can take over the rest. Once kids are safe in our shelter, God can reach out to them. It is so hard for our kids to hear God, to feel that they are loved and needed, when they are still on the streets.

Even though God's love is the best — and often the only — cure for the physical and emotional pain and abuse these kids have suffered, it's so hard for the kids to believe they're worthy of love. With your help today, we can be living examples of God's love in the lives of these children.

Can you see why this **BED AND BLANKET DRIVE** is so critical?

As this winter approaches, I'm not sure how we'll keep our covenant. And winter means more kids — which means we'll need extra clothes, extra blankets, extra heating fuel, extra electricity, and even extra food — because a child who has been shivering all day is an extra hungry child at night.

God probably won't answer my prayer to do away with winter – at least not directly. But I hope He'll at least postpone the cold weather a little. We're really in need this year, and we're not at all ready for the cold weather yet.

That's why I feel a special urgency abut this **BED & BLANKET DRIVE.** If you could send a gift in the next few days I will be so grateful.

I believe it was God who led you to Covenant House. I will always be grateful for that and I never stop thanking God for your love. Every night this winter, there will be children crying in the dark streets – lonely, cold and scared. God will hear these children and send them to us. And what you do today will make it possible for us give them all a warm, safe bed.

Chapter 5

"I was born into a gang."

"They killed him right in front of me, Sister," said 18-year-old Jeremy. "Killed him like he wasn't even human. He was driving me to school. And then, just like that, he was gone…"

I have seen hundreds of miraculous turnarounds in my first year as President of Covenant House. As I listened to Jeremy describe how his father's life came to a violent end at the hands of a rival street gang, I said a silent prayer to God for this young man to be the next Covenant House miracle.

"I was born into a gang, Sister. Both my father and my mother were gang members. But they loved me, they really did," he said. "They wanted life to be better for me. That's why they always made sure I got to school, no matter what. That's what my dad was doing, taking me to school, on the morning it happened…"

Just then, a tear formed in the eye of this tough street kid. Although he witnessed the violent death of his father over two years ago, he cannot get that terrible morning out of his mind. Who could? He has been diagnosed with post traumatic stress disorder, one of the many issues we will deal with now that Jeremy is ours.

"What happened to your mother?" I asked.

"She lost it when they killed my dad," he said. "I don't know where she is now. She just couldn't handle it..."

After witnessing his father's murder and losing touch with his mother, Jeremy turned to the only 'family' he had left. "I started running with the gang my parents belonged to," Jeremy said. "Didn't know what else to do. But I'm tired of the life, Sister. I'm just tired of it. I don't want to live on the streets anymore."

Those were the words I was praying to hear. "You don't have to live that life anymore, Jeremy," I said quickly, not wanting to miss the moment. "We have people here that can help you. We can be your family. Please stay."

Of all the wonderful things your love does for the lives of these young people, I think the greatest gift you provide is when you give us a chance to look a young man like Jeremy in the eye and say simply, "We can help you." What beautiful words to be able to tell a forgotten kid. You make it possible. I can never thank you enough for that.

We have a lot of work to do with Jeremy, but I have a dream that God willing, Jeremy will stay with us, enter our long-term residential program, and leave us a year from now, or maybe in 18 months, with a job, an apartment, and a life away from the street.

This may sound overly optimistic, but serving as President of Covenant House, I have learned that anything is possible.

Dear Lord,

This is your son. I writing you today to thank you for stopping the pain and helping me get through my ordeal that I'm facing. Help me get my life right and find a job. Amen I love you.

John, 15

Please pray for all of us at Covenant House.
May all of us find jobs and may each
one of us be at peace. I pray for those that
are sick, lonely and homeless. May they find
their way to happiness.

Charlene, 18

Chapter 6

"They come to us with numb hearts because, well, a heart can only break so many times..."

The anonymous handwritten note was left on the altar in our chapel.

"Dear God, it is Christmas Eve and <u>my heart is numb</u>. Help me through this difficult time and guide me to the right path. <u>Happy Birthday</u>."

As I spent my first Christmas with our Covenant House kids last year, I couldn't get that prayer off my mind.

When I met 17-year-old Billy, tall and skinny and alert (the other kids called him 'wired') I wondered if he left the note on the altar. Billy came to us last Christmas Eve after four months on the street and gave me a quick but unforgettable education on how to survive as a street kid...

"You keep moving, Sister," he said as his eyes darted around the room, checking out the other residents, the decorations, taking it all in, everything. "You do a lot of walking. When you can't stand the smell of yourself, you can wash up in a bus terminal bathroom. Sometimes you find a hallway or stairway to sleep in. If you can get onto a roof, that's better. You feel safer on a roof."

I told Billy how glad we were that he decided to get

off the streets and come to Covenant House for Christmas.

"Everyone just seems so happy this time of year, I figured I would see what it's like," he said. The fact Billy had to turn to a homeless shelter to find the joy of Christmas broke my heart, but I willed away the tears, hugged him and welcomed him to our family.

Was Billy the child with the numb heart?

Or was it Jane, 16 years old and alone, who timidly came up to me and asked me last Christmas Eve, "Sister, can I stay here tomorrow?" I said sure, we would love for her to stay with us. She thanked me, and said that Covenant House was the closest thing she had to a family.

Was Jane the gentle soul who wrote the prayer wishing Jesus a happy birthday while her own life was crumbling around her?

The more kids I spoke to – the more good, brave, lonely kids I spoke to – the more I came to the sad realization that any one of them could have left that prayer on the altar.

You see, almost all our kids come to us with numb hearts. Some of these kids have run away from abusive parents, some from a string of loveless foster homes. Many of them have been cast off by their families, left to fend for themselves in a world that has no place for them. *They come to us with numb hearts because, well, a heart can only break so many times...*

They will start coming to us again this year on the afternoon of December 24th, the Billys and the Janes. Many of them won't admit that they have nowhere else to go. They'll say they are just passing through and need a place to stay. They'll say they're expecting a friend to pick them up tomorrow.

What they can't say, because it's just too hard, is, "It's Christmas Eve and I don't have a friend in the world. I don't have a family that loves me, and no one else cares about me enough to share their home with me."

I think Christmas Eve is the one day of the year when the kids at Covenant House are most vulnerable. You can't pretend everything is okay when you are at a homeless shelter on Christmas Eve. You can't pretend you're cool. All the pretense at which teenagers are so good is stripped away. What is left is a lonely, tired, desperate child.

But as sad as Christmas Eve can be at Covenant House, I wouldn't miss it this year for the world. In fact, I can't wait. Because I know God has a special place in His heart for Covenant House on Christmas Eve.

I believe with all my heart that these boys and girls are precious in God's eyes. Tell that to a homeless street kid on Christmas Eve and he or she probably won't believe you. Their pasts are filled with too many lies and deceits and horrible encounters on the street. It's better if the realization that God loves them kind of creeps up on them.

And that's what will happen at Covenant House this Christmas. I've seen it with my own eyes, and it is beautiful. Last year I watched as Jane and Billy opened their presents on Christmas morning. Jane slowly, deliberately opening a brightly wrapped box, opening it like she didn't want the moment to ever fade away. And Billy, 'wired' Billy, first asking permission and then ripping open his present in record time.

Jane got a woolen hat and matching gloves, and Billy a warm, long sleeve cotton shirt. Billy immediately put on his new shirt and wore it for the rest of the day. Jane neatly put her hat and gloves back in the box, and every time I saw her that day she had the box tucked under her arm.

Those gifts, which we were able to provide only through your love and support, were more than just practical gifts for needy teenagers. Those gifts were profound reminders to these forgotten children that God loves them and you love them. Those gifts were powerful reminders to Jane and Billy that they are not alone, on Christmas or any other day of the year. And once kids start believing they are not alone — once they start believing they are loved — then miracles can happen.

Please join with me this Christmas and let's teach these kids the most important lesson they can learn. That God loves them enough — on Christmas Eve and on every other day of the year — to make their lives worth living.

Dear God, please give me the strength to go on through my stay at Covenant House. Give me the wisdom and the knowledge to do what is right and not wrong. I know I haven't been making the right decisions, but I'd like to better that. Life has not been easy through these times, but I know you will give me the strength to go on, because I do believe in you and all you say and do, Amen.

Bill, age 14

Thank you Lord, for answering my prayers. I am such an excited and happy person now. You and your miracle workers at Covenant House have given me that extra help to boost my self-esteem and build my confidence. Please continue to watch over me, Lord, in that I may continue to succeed in life.

Julie, age 17

*Dear God, thank you for my life and please help
those less fortunate than me. Thank you for
Covenant House. Thank you for the food in my
stomach and the clothes on my back.
I pray that nobody else has to go through what the
people already in Covenant House or any other
shelter have. Please bless the people who are
homeless and have no place to go.*

James, 15

Chapter 7

"It's My Mother's Ashes"

Although Kathy came to Covenant House a few years ago, I don't think any book about our kids would be complete without sharing with you her story of courage and hope...

She came to our front door on a Tuesday morning, dressed in dirty rags, holding a little aluminum paint can in her arms.

From the second she stepped inside our shelter, she mystified us. Whatever she did, wherever she went, the paint can never left her hands.

When Kathy sat in the crisis shelter, the can sat in her arms. She took the can with her to the cafeteria that first morning she ate, and to bed with her that first night she slept.

When she stepped into the shower, the can was only a few feet away. When the tiny homeless girl dressed, the can rested alongside her feet.

"I'm sorry, this is mine," she told our counselors, whenever we asked her about it. "This can belongs to me."

"Do you want to tell us what's in it, Kathy," we would ask her? "Um, not today," she said, "not today."

When Kathy was sad, or angry or hurt — which happened a lot — she took her paint can to a quiet dorm room on the 3rd floor. Sometimes she'd talk to the paint can in low whispers.

We're used to seeing many of our young people carry stuffed animals (some of the roughest, toughest kids at Covenant House have a stuffed animal.) Every kid has something — needs something — to hold.

But a paint can?

Early one morning, after Kathy had been with us a few days, I decided to "accidentally" run into her again. "Would you like to join me for breakfast?" I said. "That would be great," she said.

For a few minutes we sat in a corner of our cafeteria, talking quietly over the din of 150 ravenous homeless kids. Then I took a deep breath, and plunged into it....

"Kathy, that's a really nice can. What's in it?"

For a long time, Kathy didn't answer. She rocked back and forth, her hair swaying across her shoulders. Then she looked over at me, tears in her eyes.

"It's my mother," she said.

"Oh," I said. "What do you mean, it's your mother?" I asked.

"It's my mother's ashes," she said.

"I went and got them from the funeral home. See, I even asked them to put a label right here on the side. It has her name on it."

Kathy held the can up before my eyes. A little label on the side chronicled all that remained of her mother: date of birth, date of death, name. That was it. Then Kathy pulled the can close, and hugged it.

"I never really knew my mother, Sister," Kathy told me. "I mean, she threw me in the garbage two days after I was born." (We checked Kathy's story. Sure enough the year Kathy was born, the New York newspapers ran a story, saying that police had found a little infant girl in a dumpster ... and yes, it was two days after Kathy was born.)

"I ended up living in a lot of foster homes, mad at my mother," Kathy said. "But then, I decided I was going to try to find her. I got lucky — someone knew where she was living. I went to her house."

"She wasn't there, Sister," she said. "My mother was in the hospital. She had AIDS. She was dying.

"I went to the hospital, and I got to meet her the day before she died. My mother told me she loved me, Sister," Kathy said crying. "She told me she loved me." (We double-checked Kathy's story ... every word of it was true.)

I reached out and hugged Kathy, and she cried in my arms for a long, long time. It was tough getting my arms around her, because she just wouldn't put the paint can down. But she didn't seem to mind. I know I didn't...

I saw Kathy again, later that day, eating dinner in our cafeteria. She made a point to come up and say hi. I made a point to give her an extra hug...

I feel like crying whenever I think of Kathy. I can't seem to stop feeling this way. I guess this story — the whole horrible, sad, unreal mess — hurts too much.

I guess that's why I just had to write you this letter.

I need to ask you something very important, and I'm praying you'll consider it, if you can.

Do you think you could help kids like Kathy ... and the new and desperate kids who will come to our shelter this week? Please?

There's one very important thing you need to know about Covenant House and our kids and it is this — A DONATION TO COVENANT HOUSE IS THE ABSOLUTE BEST WAY YOU CAN HELP THE TERRIFIED AND HELPLESS HOMELESS KIDS ON OUR STREETS!

> This year more than 80,000 homeless kids ... kids who are 15, 16, 17 years old ... will come to our doors.
>
> We'll give these kids food, and a safe bed to sleep in (the streets are incredibly dangerous!) and medicine, and counseling if they need it (most kids do.)
>
> But most of all, we'll give these kids love. For thousands of these kids, the love we give them tonight will be the first love they've ever known!

We are here for kids like Kathy 24 hours a day, in cities across America, 365 days a year. No kid — no kid! — is ever turned away ever!

Thanks to the love and help of thousands of caring people — people just like you — Covenant House spends MORE than the entire federal government to help these kids. (That's what I meant when I said that giving to us is THE best way to help these kids.)

But so much more needs to be done. And we simply can't do it alone.

Chapter 8

"She's a Cutter..."

She came to us on a winter night wearing only jeans and a thin t-shirt, and holding a newspaper over her head in a futile attempt to keep the wet snow out of her hair.

Her name was Jenny and looking past a fading black eye you could see she was really quite beautiful. She asked:

"Can I come in just for a minute to get warm?"

"Of course," was our answer, *"You look like you're freezing. How about a hot shower and some dry clothes, some soup or hot cocoa and a bed for the rest of the night where you can be warm and safe?"*

Never in my wildest imagination could I have predicted her reply.

"I better not, Sister. I'm bad news ... just no good at all."

She wasn't ready yet to tell us what she meant by that, but thankfully we were successful in convincing her to stay with us that night. And the next day she came downstairs for breakfast, and then went back to her room. Later that morning, I received a very disturbing emergency alert about her.

"She's a cutter," I was told.

I knew what that meant. Every now and then one of the kids who comes to us has been so traumatized that they suffer from a psychological disorder where they'll take a sharp object of some kind and make marks and cuts on their arms and legs.

I was worried that if we didn't help her, and quickly, there was a danger that soon the other kids might be making fun of her and ridiculing her, or even be fearful of her. So I dropped everything and had a long heart-to-heart talk with Jenny. What she told me she'd been through is utterly unthinkable, it's that awful.

Her problem began when she was, maybe, about 12 years old or so, as far as we could tell. Jenny probably matured early and looked much older than she was at the time. And like most girls her age, she was experimenting with make-up and hair styles, eager to fit in and be liked by the kids in her class.

Then, one afternoon when only Jenny and her father were at home, "it" happened, she told me in a whisper. **Jenny was raped by her own father.**

She was so ashamed and scared she couldn't bring herself to tell anyone. Then it happened again one night when everyone else was asleep. When it happened a third time she finally got up the courage to tell her mother.

And the response she received?

"You're making it all up. All of it. It isn't true."

My heart broke for Jenny at the same time I filled with anger at what was done to her. However, so far her story was fairly typical. In fact, tragically typical. Rape by a parent or stepparent happens more times than we want to imagine. The American Academy of Pediatrics reports that one out of five girls is a victim of sexual abuse in childhood and 80% of the time it's someone she knows and trusts or loves. <u>But there was more</u>.

Next she was raped by, of all people, her own grandfather. So at this point, her father knew what was going on, and so did her grandfather, and her mother continued to deny the truth. That was only the beginning. An uncle who lived not far away also raped her. As did a cousin.

Imagine, if you can, this poor child, repeatedly sexually assaulted, and violated, and demeaned, and betrayed by the very individuals in her family who should have respected and protected and comforted and loved her, and all without any concern from her mother.

<u>Just where is the breaking point when a child suffers this much trauma</u>? The answer came to the surface when she told me:

> *"You know, it was all my fault. I always wanted to wear make-up like the popular girls at school and dress nice. I shouldn't have tried to be pretty. That's my fault, Sister."*

That was why she cut herself. In her tormented way of thinking she figured that if she could scar herself and make herself look ugly, then men would leave her alone. She took the blame on herself.

As I've been reflecting on Jesus' life and death since Lent began last week, Jenny's story reminded me of the terrible agony Jesus went through in the time leading up to the Crucifixion. Jesus had been betrayed and beaten. Those close to Jesus had fled away, while those who stood by Jesus' side responded with cowardly denial. God's great love was sufficient for Jesus. As it is for Jenny, if we can help her understand that she can be free of the blame — that nothing that happened to her is her fault. It will be a long journey for Jenny, and she's going to need us every step of the way.

I pledge to you, that with help from friends like you, especially during this season of Lent, we'll give Jenny all the love and care she needs.

We don't want her to leave us. She can't go back home, because nothing awaits her there but a mother who denied her and family members who repeatedly raped her.

She knows there's no future for her on the streets, because nothing awaits her there but an army of pimps, drug dealers and pornographers who all want a piece of her. They'll make her sell her body, run drugs, you name it.

The plain fact is that kids on the streets have to do everything they can to survive. Thank God, the instinct to stay alive is so strong.

We want Jenny to survive right here with us. We want to surround her with unconditional love. We want to cheer her on as she makes progress, and if she slips and falters, we want to be here when she needs us the most. It's not going to be easy for her.

*God, I have made so many mistakes in life, but I'm
learning at Covenant House that there are ways to
keep trying instead of giving up. I'm still trying not
to be sucked into the life on the street.
God, please accept me.*

Carol, 17

Chapter 9

Learning to fly...

I just witnessed the greatest graduation ceremony I've ever seen. Over 300 young people — formerly homeless kids who could have easily been lost to the streets forever —instead participated in a graduation ceremony at our Covenant House shelter, wearing caps and gowns and unabashed pride on their faces that lit up the room.

All 300 of these heroic kids could have easily disappeared into the streets, victims of a silent but violent war that is being fought nightly on the streets of our cities. We could have lost them all before their 18th birthdays.

They could have given in to despair, to the hopelessness into which they were born. They could have looked around, saw other children with loving homes and families, decided life just wasn't fair, and quit. Or turned to crime. Or drugs.

Instead, these young people, these 300 heroes, accepted that life is unfair. And instead of quitting, instead of turning to crime or prostitution or drugs, they said, "So what. I'll make it on my own." And they found their way to Covenant House.

Their courage, their incredible will to survive against all odds, is the reason they are graduates of our long-term residential program we call Rights of Passage.

I couldn't be prouder if they were my own children. I hope you feel the same way, because in many ways they are your children as well.

They certainly could not have received the life-saving help they got at Covenant House if not for the love and support from friends like you.

Our Rights of Passage program is based on the simple belief that all children have the right to pass into adulthood without being abused and homeless. I could go on to give you a clinical description of the program, but it took me about two days on the job to learn that the young people describe their experiences better than I ever could. And so let me share with you what one of our Rights of Passage graduates told me the program means to him.

"When I first came to Covenant House, I saw a big picture painted on the wall of a dove resting in a hand. It's their logo, but it also tells the story of what Covenant House is all about. As a resident of Rights of Passage, you are that bird and the program is one big nest. In this nest there are a lot of helpers – the staff, your mentor, the people who send money, the other kids in the program. The nest is like a family, but it's also a classroom. You're always learning something you need to finally make it. And the great thing is – when you go out on a ledge, and even if you fall a

few times, there's always someone there to catch you and say, 'it's ok, try again.' And when you're ready, when the pieces are in place, there's encouragement of all kinds to help you take off and really FLY.'

Pretty great young man. Thank you for helping us teach him how to fly.

Please help this month if you can. The thousands of children who will be sleeping on the streets of our cities tonight are not dreaming of graduation ceremonies, or of new jobs or new apartments. Most of their dreams will focus on surviving until tomorrow morning.

But tonight, our outreach counselors will be on the streets, providing food, clothing and counseling. Tonight, God willing, a forgotten street child will come into our shelter and begin the incredible journey that will lead to a cap, a gown, and a future off the street.

Dear Lord, I thank you for allowing me to find this place. I thank you for blessing me to be able to pass my test for my job. I hope and wish that you guide me through the hard times that my family members and I are going through.

Cindy, 16

Chapter 10

"Covenant House is their last hope. That's the reality. It's that sad and it's that simple."

I had just returned to my office from a very long and stressful budget meeting that was very short on good news.

I was sitting at my desk fighting off a rare but quite powerful "what-have-I-gotten-myself-into" moment when my mind flashed back to a conversation I had with a well-meaning Covenant House friend a few days before.

"Sister Tricia, I know it's tough raising money these days and there are more homeless kids than ever," he said. "I've got an idea that will raise you a ton of money."

My friend now had my undivided attention.

"What if you allowed a television network to prop up some cameras on the street outside the front door of the Covenant House Crisis Shelter?

"It would be the ultimate 'reality show,' wouldn't it?" he said, his eyes flashing with excitement. "Children, left all on their own, on the dangerous streets, with nothing but the clothes on their backs. Criminals, drug dealers, pimps, waiting for them, hoping to use the children's bodies for profit.

"Ratings would be huge, advertising revenue from the show would pour in…"

I cut my friend off before he started talking movie deals. I told him I really appreciated his support, but that the covenant we make with every child who comes through our door is a sacred trust, based on unconditional love and confidentiality. I told him I would never allow our children to be used in this way.

I must admit, though, the idea of millions of people seeing what we see at the front door of Covenant House every night did appeal to me. Instead of a faceless, forgotten army, millions of television viewers would start to see street children as human beings. As brave, spirited young people who have survived abuse and neglect and family disintegration. As young children who desperately need help.

Last night, our Crisis Shelter was running as smoothly as a 24-hour, no-questions-asked crisis shelter smack in the middle of the dangerous streets ever could or would. Here is a brief report from the front lines, straight from the intake desk. Only the names of the children have been changed.

Teresa, age 16, comes in with tears running down her once pretty, now badly bruised face. She was attacked by a gang at the bus terminal – the police officer from the emergency room brought her to us.

Bill opens the door tentatively. He's obviously a shy kid, and anxious. It takes 20 minutes for him to express his worry that he won't be able to breathe — he's asthmatic, and his inhaler was in his backpack that was stolen while he slept under an overpass.

Jack, 18, comes in, silent at first, then says he is thinking of killing himself, has nowhere else to go and doesn't care what happens to him...

Everett, 18, 6'3", has been on the streets for three years and is now involved in a gang; says he wants help to get out of the life...

Sharon, 16, had been living with her sister but they got into a fight and she has been "working" on the streets the past three months. She was beat up by some other girls and does not want to go back out there. Staff took her to the clinic for a physical and emotional check up.

Christopher, has been living on the street for a year, comes to our crisis shelter regularly but won't stay. Came in high yesterday, unable to stand, focus or speak clearly. His pulse was taken and staff decided to transport him to the Emergency Room. Staff stayed with Christo-

pher at the Emergency Room until 2 am, when he was released and staff brought back to Covenant House. We will try again to convince him to stay with us...

Young people like Teresa and Bill and John and Everett and Sharon and Christopher and hundreds like them are victims of a poverty-stricken, tragic lifestyle that takes away hope and purpose and dreams and goals. They come to us in crisis, as a last resort, actually believing that they belong on the streets. They will keep believing that and will disappear into those streets unless somebody helps them.

That "somebody" is us. Covenant House is their last hope. That's the reality. It's that sad and it's that simple.

There are 1700 children sleeping in our shelters tonight. Help from friends like you is the only reason we didn't have to say no to any of them.

Tonight, at our crisis shelters across America, hundreds of children who have never been told they are worthwhile will hear it; who've never felt the warmth of a fellow human being's affection will feel it; who've never known love will find it. That is why immediate Crisis Care, 24 hours a day, seven days a week, is and always will be the cornerstone of what we do here at Covenant House.

Of all the things we do here at Covenant House to help street children, it all starts with Crisis Care. It all starts with a hungry, desperate child at the end of his or her rope in the middle of the night, swallowing their last bit of pride and walking in off the streets and into our Crisis Shelter and saying, "Help me. Please."

Last night, by the grace of God, Teresa and Bill and Jack and Everett and Sharon and Christopher found the courage to come in off the streets and ask for help. What an absolute tragedy it would have been if they made that decision and we weren't here for them.

But we were, thanks to you. And we will be here tonight. And we will work very hard to keep these children off the streets, to show them they are loved, and convince them that their lives matter.

*Dear Lord, today is my last day at Covenant House.
I want to thank you for helping me get through this.
You made me stronger than I was before.
Now that I'm leaving, please look out for me.
I'm a little scared. Please help me get through this
next change in my life. I love you. Amen*

Charles, age 20

Chapter 11

Adam was five when his father sold him as a sex toy...

Have you ever wondered if the work we do at Covenant House *really* helps our kids?

To be honest, there are times when I wonder that myself. The kids who knock on our door at night are often dealing with such serious issues that sometimes I feel like the help we offer can never, ever be enough.

But that's usually when God sends along a teenager like Adam. He lets me know that, by working together, <u>you and I really *are* making a difference</u>. Your compassionate support allows us to offer shelter, guidance and healing to teens like him who have been hurt very deeply.

Adam came to Covenant House after his mom kicked him out. They'd had a fight and he'd been living on the streets. He didn't tell me a lot about himself at first, but then a lot of our kids don't. They need to take it slow and see if they can really trust us.

So I gave Adam the time he needed. He started dropping by my office every now and then to chat. He was a very polite kid and a real whiz with computers. He also enrolled in our culinary arts job-training class that we offer to older teens through our Rights of Passage program.

On the surface, Adam seemed to be doing fine. He seemed to enjoy his culinary arts class, but I was starting to get concerned about him. Emotionally he was very withdrawn.

Then I learned that Adam always slept in his clothes. In fact, he even wore his sneakers to bed.

That raised a big red flag for me. I gently tried to get Adam to open up about his problems. He didn't want to at first. He was so ashamed of what had happened that he didn't want anybody to know about it. But he'd kept his secret locked inside for so long that he couldn't hide it anymore. Eventually he told me his painful story...

His dad was a crack addict. He let his buddies use Adam as a sex toy in exchange for drugs. <u>The first time it happened, Adam was just 5 years old</u>!

That's why Adam started sleeping in his clothing. It was the only way he could think of to protect himself. **He was so young he actually thought he'd be safe if he kept his clothes and shoes on.**

It went on like that for years. Adam never knew when his dad would drag him out of bed at night and let his friends take turns on him. But the worst part was when Adam told me he felt like he must have done something to deserve it. He felt like he should have been able to fight back.

I did my best to explain to him that what happened wasn't his fault. There was simply no way a little boy could protect himself from a fully grown man. But for the life of me I couldn't explain to him why <u>his mom never once tried to protect him</u> from being raped.

I know a lot of the kids here at Covenant House have been hurt in pretty awful ways, but I'm having a hard time getting Adam's story out of my mind. I keep thinking about all the other boys and girls on the streets that we haven't been able to reach yet.

How many of them have gone through the same things Adam did? How many of them feel so ashamed and dirty inside they think they deserve every ugly thing that happened to them?

I'm sure you'd agree with me that <u>no child should be forgotten on the streets and left to suffer such terrible hurt and shame alone</u>.

I don't mean to remind you of all the sad things that can happen to unwanted children. But I just can't help myself. I care about these kids so much – and I believe you do too – that it breaks my heart to see them in such pain. I want to gather up all these homeless, unloved children and bring them to Covenant House to keep them safe.

But I started out this letter to tell you good news.

You've been incredibly generous to our boys and girls, and I want to be sure you know what a difference you make in their lives.

While he was here, Adam worked hard to deal with his shame and anger about what happened to him. He began making friends and he did very well in his culinary arts program. That gave his self-confidence a real shot in the arm!

<u>I knew Adam had reached a turning point when he stopped sleeping in his clothes and sneakers</u>. He realized he didn't need to protect himself that way anymore.

He knew he was finally safe.

Adam didn't stop there. It took time, but he finished his GED and got a job in a local restaurant.

Not long ago, he even moved into his own apartment. You might not think these achievements are particularly remarkable. But to teens who have been abused the way Adam was – and whose self-worth is so low they can barely even scrape it off the floor – they are <u>triumphs</u>.

Adam knows how far he's come. When he first arrived here, he had hidden his feelings for so long he couldn't even find words to express himself. Today, he's an articulate speaker and an inspiration to the other kids in the program.

"I never would have been able to even begin to rebuild my life with small, simple steps," he said recently, *"without the assistance of Covenant House."*

I wanted to share his comments with you so you know how much of a difference you make. Your support allows us to offer safety and healing to boys and girls who have been abused in terrible ways.

I feel blessed to know that we have caring friends like you by our side. And I pray you will help us continue this vital work by making another generous gift. Your faithful support will give our children the help they need to rebuild their lives – one small, simple step at a time.

Adam drops in every now and then to tell me how well he's doing. Every time I see him, he reminds me that <u>even when kids have been hurt so deeply, there's still hope</u>. They have a better future ahead.

All they need is a helping hand from decent, compassionate people like you who care about them. You literally help them build new lives.

Chapter 12

*"They made me keep the
handcuffs on..."*

"I think you better see this kid, Sister Tricia," said
Yolanda.

I had just returned from a week of speaking engage-
ments, talking to any group willing to listen about our
children. I was ready for any food that didn't resemble
airplane cuisine, and then I had a date with a bunch of
almost overdue bills. But when Yolanda called, I knew
to put everything else aside.

You see, Yolanda works at our front door. Yolanda
is the first person a kid sees when they come in off the
street, and the impression she makes lasts forever.

She is the reason a lot of children decide to leave
the streets and stay with us. She is dedicated and smart
and loves these children with all her heart and I believe God sent her to us.

"Sister, I would like you to meet Stephen," said
Yolanda, and I was struck immediately by the sadness
in the young man's eyes. Actually, it went beyond
sadness, to a physical kind of shame he seemed to be
carrying. Head down, shoulders slumped, arms limp.

"Hi Stephen," I said, and, as I offered my hand, his
eyes never left the carpet.

"They made me keep the handcuffs on for the whole ride, Sister," he almost whispered. "I wish they didn't have to do that."

"I'm sorry, Stephen," I said. "That must have been terrible. No more handcuffs, I promise," I said.

I sensed this wasn't the time to ask Stephen a lot of questions about his past. I knew from Yolanda that Stephen never met his father, and that his mother has been a drug addict since before he was born.

I knew Stephen was living on the streets at age 15 when he stole some money for food. I knew that very bad mistake had cost him the last two years in an upstate juvenile detention center.

And I knew one more thing — our job now was to make sure the mistake Stephen made as a scared, hungry, all-alone 15-year-old doesn't lead to a death sentence on the streets.

"I don't know why they brought me here, Sister" he said. "It looks like a nice place and all. But there's nothing you can do for me."

"I know things don't look great now, but we can help you, Stephen," I said. "Please stay. There are a lot of people here who care about you.

"Stay with us, please," I said again, and this time he took his eyes off the carpet and looked me almost in the eye. It was a start.

I honestly don't know what will become of Stephen. What I do know is that he is a beautiful creation of God, someone who has been denied the basic things every child deserves; the knowledge that he is worthy and good and priceless and loved.

Stephen is ours now. We will love him unconditionally, and we'll be able to give him all the tools he needs to succeed — thanks to you. And we will pray very hard that the same incredible spirit which has kept this young man alive through his 17-year-nightmare-of-a-life can be re-kindled when he is surrounded by people who love him.

I pray Stephen will make it. I pray he will stay with us. I think he will, because of Yolanda. Because of the rest of the wonderful caring staff God has sent to Covenant House. And because of you, who I also believe God has sent to us.

Beyond any possible way of saying it, I am grateful to you for loving Stephen and every one of the almost 80,000 children we will serve this year. Without you and your consistent support, we simply would have to close our doors.

Dear Lord, I need your help right now things aren't going right with me. I need you to lead me into the right direction. Thank you.

Sandy, 18

Chapter 13

"He's Going to Kill Me."

Lanie is one of the girls I'll never forget. She came to Covenant House at about 4 o'clock one cold morning, with her right eye almost completely swollen shut and a split lip. She barely whispered:

"Help me. Please help me. He's going to kill me."

We could guess who the "he" was — her pimp. Clearly this one was violent, controlling Lanie by terrorizing her.

Her sleeveless silver mini-dress was torn and the strap of one of her high heels had broken off. We bundled her up quickly in a couple of thick, warm blankets as we listened to her story.

"I asked him if I could put on a coat since it was almost morning and there weren't any guys around. He beat me for even asking. But I couldn't help it. I was freezing cold.

"And now since I ran, I know he's going to hunt me like an animal. I'm so scared, Sister."

Beyond his physical abuse and psychological control over her, Lanie was completely dependent on him for her food and her clothing, and her very life. We knew right away it wasn't going to be easy for her to break free from his death-grip on her, but we were determined to help.

Upstairs, we tended her battered face, gave her a toiletry kit and a pair of pajamas, then tucked her into bed after she showered and changed.

Lanie didn't sleep long. She came downstairs for breakfast, and then paced around the building, restless and edgy. Worried, I'm sure, about what the pimp would do to her if he found her.

It's hard for you and me to understand, but a pimp's control over a girl is <u>complete and total</u>.

It's almost as though the girl loses all sense of herself and has no free will ... the pimp decides everything for her.

After a couple of days, Lanie settled down and started talking to some of the other kids. That was a really encouraging sign. We prayed and prayed she would stay with us and let us help her reclaim her life and her future.

Gradually, Lanie opened up to us. She told us that her mother was a crack addict and slowly dying.

Lanie's earliest memory is that of people coming to her house and giving her mother money, and her mother giving them stuff in little bags. Of course the bags were full of drugs, though she didn't understand it at the time.

She even remembered once when the police came and people started shooting guns, and her mother was put in jail for a couple of years.

During that time, Lanie lived in a foster home where she was sexually abused. She ran away to escape the repeated assaults, thinking like a lot of kids do that anything would be better than that.

But like millions of kids who run away or get thrown out of their homes, Lanie fell prey to a very cunning pimp that very same day.

Statistically — and this is shocking but absolutely true — **runaway girls find themselves under the control of a pimp <u>within 48 hours</u> of leaving home.** Lanie was no different.

Pimps use stealthy manipulation tactics to gain girls' trust. These days, they're casually dressed just like any other guy their age (mostly about 20) and they strike up a conversation and quickly figure out how to become the girl's fantasy boyfriend.

They flatter her, offer friendship and a shoulder to cry on. But the next thing she knows, the pimp has her turning tricks and "paying him back" for all his "help."

Like Lanie said one day,

"He's the only person who ever took care of me ... he told me he loved me all the time. And

he showed me how to make money when men came out of strip clubs, how to offer them a 'date.' He made it all sound so glamorous and like I was in control, why shouldn't I make money?"

Obviously, her pimp was a master at sweet talk — promising he'd take care of her and that he loved her. Oh, the promise of being loved is such a powerful, irresistible draw for young girls like Lanie who are desperate for someone ... anyone ... to care for them.

"It's just a bunch of lies," we told her, *"You know that, deep down. He doesn't love you. If he really loved you, he wouldn't put you out on the street."*

"I know you're probably right. But I really needed him, and at first he did seem like he loved me. He used to give me little presents all the time, like a necklace or perfume. Nobody ever gave me a gift before him."

My heart broke for her and I completely understood how her pimp's attention filled her desperate yearning to be loved. It was all-encompassing.

I'll never know what depths of despair drove her to it, but a few days later, we found Lanie slumped in the bathroom. She had just drank a full bottle of Tilex.

"I want to die. Please, just let me die," she pleaded.

We rushed her to the emergency room, and were indescribably relieved when the doctor said we got her there in time and she would survive. He said she was very weak and needed to rest, but she would recover.
 A few hours later, we learned from the hospital staff, Lanie slipped out of bed, put on her clothes, walked down the back stairs of the hospital, and disappeared.

Just vanished.

I wake up in the dark of night sometimes and wonder if she's thinking about Covenant House, and thinking about coming back to us — and I pray God will lead her here.

Where else will she get the psychological guidance she needs? And how else will she ever finish high school?

We can put her in our Rights of Passage program, where she can learn independent living skills, and get the practical skills she needs to lead a full and productive adulthood — so that her choices in life won't be limited to those of a prostitute.

And Lanie is just one heartbreaking reason why I must continue writing to special friends like you, urging you to send another gift of love, so that we can keep our doors open 24 hours a day, and be here when a kid needs us most.

Maybe someday Lanie's story will have a happy ending. I've seen kids walk through our door with more problems than you can ever imagine. And then after they've experienced the love and care and counseling that we provide them, many make a complete and total turnaround.

I pray it happens for Lanie.

Dear God, I wish I could change some things that I've done. My life is so empty, I am missing something. I pray if you could make my days better I would really appreciate that.

Mark, 14

God, I pray I see my parents one day because they both died in 1993. I pray that some day I live in peace.

Bill, 18

Dear God, I praise you, please be with me tomorrow as I go to my job interview. I love you amen.

Maggie, 20

Dear Lord, please touch all who are suffering and grieving.

Anonymous note left in our chapel

*Dear God, please don't take my father away.
He's all I have left. I know my mom is up
there with you. Please help me. I can't stay
being depressed. I'm homeless
and I can't believe this. Pray for my father
to stop drinking. I don't want him to die.
I need him.*

Trevor, age 17

Chapter 14

"Reality hit me ...
I was 15 and a runaway..."

"When I ran to the streets, I made friends with a guy who was my age. He told me that he'd survived on the streets by turning tricks. I was so naive, I thought he was talking about juggling, like in the circus or something ... I had a lot to learn."

Bess, 15

"I was from this middle-class family. I had every material thing I wanted, Sister," said Bess. "But I wasn't going back home. I didn't care if I lived or died. My father was a drunk and he beat me, and my mother didn't want to get my father mad, so she just chose to let the beatings happen. I wasn't going back. I just couldn't."

Bess ran to the streets, where she found it only took a couple of days of being all alone and utterly homeless and lost to come to terms with the fact that life on the streets is a dead end. And that she could very well end up dead.

"I found Covenant House, and when I first got to your shelter, I was really lost," Bess remembers. "I was standing in this room I'd been assigned and the reality hit me: I'm a runaway. I'm 15 and I'm a good person. What's going on?"

There really isn't a "profile" of the typical Covenant House kid. But the one thing they have in common, whether they are a boy or a girl or from the suburbs or the city. They've all got one sure thing in common: They don't have anywhere else to go.

Covenant House is it, the last stop, the end of the line, their last and only hope.

They come in with black eyes and broken hearts, bleeding and torn. Some come in with a swagger and a cold stare — others shaking non-stop and unable to speak or look you in the eye.

And especially when the nights are cold and no matter what they do they can't get out of the rain, they come in sick as dogs, burning up with a fever and so weak they can barely stand.

Some kids have been through such horror on the streets at the hands of pimps who beat them into submission and terror, and johns who think that for a few bucks the kid they've just "purchased" is theirs to violate and denigrate and slap around, too.

After a while, the kids lose all sense of self ... never mind any feeling of worth or ability or value. They know they're just a commodity.

They feel like they are like the living dead. They wish they were dead for real, until even that is gone and they're just utterly empty inside.

That's what the streets do to our kids.

All kids make mistakes or exercise poor judgment from time to time, and ones like Bess who become runners are most vulnerable in some ways. They don't have the street smarts of chronically abused kids, usually.

Today, Bess knows how lucky she was that she'd somehow managed to escape a pimp's reach, that she hadn't been abducted like thousands of girls are every day, disappearing into an underworld of sexual slavery and an inevitable violent death or a death sentence in the form of disease.

Where is the light for these kids?

In us, here at Covenant House, as we show and share and shine God's love just as bright and strong as we can.

I keep thinking, with Easter just around the corner, that in a way, we are their Easter.

They come to us just about dead, buried deep, deep in sorrow and despair, psychically wounded and beyond hurt.

But with time, and patience, and complete and unconditional love and support, they can experience a resurrection.

One day at a time, one encouraging smile at a time, day by day they rise.

Like Bess. It wasn't easy, but she followed the rules (You bet, just like families everywhere, we have them and they're enforced!), she pitched in to do chores, and she got up at the crack of dawn every day to catch the bus to school. She did her homework when she got back, and she got a job at McDonald's when she turned 16.

Thankfully, an aunt and uncle agreed to have Bess come live with them. We gave her a bus ticket and packed her off with our love and our fingers crossed. Bess struggled, but ultimately managed to finish high school and her future looks bright.

But truthfully, every day is a struggle for us to keep up with the financial realities of keeping our doors open every day of the year, 24 hours a day.

That's why I am so profoundly grateful to you. Your generous gifts put food on our table, gas in our Outreach Vans, and you keep this roof over our heads.

Do you know what a miracle that is?

You are our miracle-maker, the source of our ability to mend broken hearts and battered bodies and souls ... to give kids the Easter in their own lives that God wants so much for them.

Because of you, every day has a little Easter in it, inside the walls of Covenant House.

Yes, because of you, resurrection is possible for some of the most lost and hurting kids on earth who've been given up for dead.

You are nothing less than God's love in action, sharing the heavenly promise of hope and new life with boys and girls God especially loves ... the children of the streets.

*Hello Lord, thank you for allowing me
to see another day.
I hope to see many more. I pray to get accepted
into a job program so that I can start to better
my life and keep up my responsibilities.*

Matt, 18

*Dear God, I pray that my brothers and sisters
are grateful that they are not
sleeping on the streets tonight.
Thank you for this place.*

Jeremy, 18

Chapter 15

"Sometimes I hope the next bullet has my name on it..."

He said his name was "T." Just "T."

"That's right, Sister Tricia, it's nothing more than one letter. But that 'T' is enough for me — it's my street name."

Reading between the lines, I knew this "street name" was gang-related.

"Do you mean that's what the other guys in the gang call you?" I asked.

"They do, yeah, but it's the only name I ever had that I can remember," T said.

"What do you mean, T?"

I asked him casually, knowing I had to tread gently with this kid or he'd bolt.

"I dunno," he said, *"I mean, I've been on the streets since I was, like, eight or nine years old, I guess.*

"I don't remember much before that ... obviously I had to have had parents or I wouldn't be here. But I don't remember them or where we lived or anything."

Eight or nine! I've worked with a lot of troubled kids and I've seen all kinds of abuse but, thank God, it's extremely rare for a child who's only eight or nine to end up on the streets for any length of time.

For T, that was years ago. He was a teenager now.

To hear him talk about it, though, it seems like his life prior to being on the streets was decades and decades ago, the memories faded until they were all but gone. In fact, I suspect T's mind may have blocked out the details of his earliest years, either because it was so bad then, or because of what had happened to him in the ensuing years on the streets.

Either way, this was one young man with a heap of problems.

"Tell me about what you can remember, T," I said softly.

"You're not going to like it, Sister," he said.

"That's all right, T. We don't judge anybody here — we know you have to do what you have to do to survive on the streets," I assured him. *"I'd never hold that against you, ever."*

So over the next hour or so, as we talked in a quiet corner of the cafeteria over a cup of hot cocoa, I came to realize that it was an utter miracle that T was alive, sitting right there in front of me.

He should be dead. He should have died years ago, in fact.

That's what gang life does to kids. They live with the threat of imminent violence — deadly violence — every day. They get caught up in drugs and stealing and all manner of criminal activity.

It's easy to blame them and say they're bad to the core, that they deserve bad things to happen to them.

What's harder to do is understand how we (their parents and other adults in their lives, and we as a society) have failed them.

Now, I'm not saying I condone gang activity of any kind, please don't misunderstand. Yet the reality is that a lot of kids end up in gangs because they don't have strong parental guidance at home, particularly during the most difficult growing-up years when they need it most.

I believe the allure of gangs is especially strong for boys whose dads do a disappearing act and whose mothers are worked to the bone, exhausted, and it's all they can do to keep it together. Disciplining pre-adolescent and adolescent boys is never easy.

And as troubles mount at home, one of two things typically happen. Either mom can't take the acting out and the bad behavior anymore and shows her kid the door, or the kid refuses to abide by household rules and has this fantasy that life on the streets with his friends will be the freedom he seeks.

If T had first found himself on the streets at 14 or 15 or 16, either of those scenarios might sound familiar to him.

As I sat there listening to T, I didn't see a hardened teenager before me or a terrible kid ... I saw his innocence and I imagined what he must have looked like at eight.

I mourned for that little boy, for what was done to him.

How in the world could anyone turn a kid who's still just a baby out on the streets like someone had done to him?

Working with homeless kids, I've come to accept that sometimes you just never get the answers you seek. I also know that God has placed these children in our care because our love does not require answers. We give the kids our love freely and unconditionally, always.

That wasn't hard with T. He's one of those kids who's been so scarred by events in his life that he somehow came to the conclusion that he didn't deserve to be loved.

Sure, he talked about how the gang is his "family" and they've "got each other's backs," but I sat there thinking, *"No wonder you think that's love, T, because you've never known the love of a real family."*

I didn't say that, of course. Mostly, I just listened. T told me about how the gang took him in right away and that he doesn't remember life before them.

"But I'm not proud, Sister. I mean, I've done some really awful things. I've never killed anybody, but some things ... well, I don't want to talk about it.

"I hate myself. Sometimes I hope the next bullet or knife has my name on it," T admitted, almost whispering.

"To tell you the truth, Sister, my head's down so low I can't even pick it up by myself anymore."

Oh, how my heart ached for him. I was happy beyond words when he let me hug him as I promised he had come to the right place and we will do everything in the world to help him turn his life around into something he can be proud of. I wondered how long it had been since anybody hugged him, because it seemed like he didn't want to let go. I held him and held him for the longest time.

It wasn't until the next morning that I realized he'd been saying goodbye. He was gone, back to the streets and a gang he's terrified to try to escape.

I can't get him out of my mind. I'm praying for him, praying God will lead him back to us, praying T will give us a chance to help him.

Please pray for T tonight, even though you've never met him and probably never will. He's a really special kid, really special ... an eight year-old who never had a chance.

Dear Lord, I am having a difficult time in life right now. I need a job really badly and I need the help of your guidance to show me down the path that will help me get a good job. I have been trying with some success but I know that once you step in I will accomplish all success. Thank you Lord for giving me a clear mind, in that I have not been thinking of taking my own life. Thank you for giving me a chance to see different things in life when I go on the Covenant House trips. Please keep a close eye on me, God.

Michael, 19

Chapter 16

"Footprints"

This morning, I walked downstairs from my office to the shelter and watched as hundreds of kids – young people who have been rescued from the streets – got ready to go to school or a job-training program. I watched them eat warm breakfasts. I saw young mothers hugging their babies.

In the midst of this beautiful bedlam, I met Julie, a 16-year-old who pulled me aside and thanked me for running Covenant House. "If it wasn't for this place, I would still be on the streets, or maybe even dead," she said matter-of-factly.

I told Julie how happy I was that she found Covenant House, and told her she was part of our family now. As we spoke, I noticed a card sticking out of her pocket.

"My counselor gave it to me, it was sent in by someone who donates to Covenant House," Julie explained. "It is signed, 'God bless you, love, Rose.' I thought it was real nice of this Rose lady to send it so I thought I would save it," said Julie.

I recognized the card as one we sent to some of our friends a few months back. It is called "Foot-prints" and I think it says everything about what you mean to our kids:

"One night I dreamed I was walking along the beach with the Lord. Many scenes from my life flashed across the sky. In each scene I noticed footprints in the sand.

Sometimes there were two sets of footprints. Other times there were only one set of footprints. This bothered me because I noticed that during the low periods of my life, I could only see one set of footprints. So I said to the Lord, "You promised me, Lord, that if I followed You, You would walk with me always. But I noticed that during the most trying periods of my life, there is only one set of prints in the sand. Why, when I have needed You the most, have You abandoned me?"

The Lord replied, "My child, I love you and would never leave you. The times when you have seen only one set of footprints are the times when I carried you."

Your love and support gives us the incredible opportunity to pick these children up in God's loving arms and carry them through the unspeakable hardships they face in their young lives. I can never thank you enough for that.

I feel privileged that God has put me here in this place and given me the chance to help these kids who are so desperate and have no place else to go. I do it in partnership with you and with God, always. As concerned as I am, it helps more than I can ever tell you to know that you're there for these precious children when they need you most. I never, ever stop thanking God that you found us.

*Covenant House is like a family, with
all a family's ups and downs. But the
really great thing about being here is
that I'm never lonely anymore. There's
always someone here, no matter what time,
to talk to. And that makes a big difference
when you're trying to build a life for yourself.*

James, 18

Chapter 17

"Your outreach workers saved my life."

Not long ago, I received a letter from a young man we once helped, named Dennis. His words said better than I ever could what a difference you make to runaway and abandoned kids.

A few years back, I was a homeless teenager eating out of dumpsters on the streets, when the shiny blue Covenant House van pulled up and offered me a free bag lunch with a peanut butter sandwich. I will never forget how hungry I was, and how good that sandwich tasted. Looking back, I think I can say your outreach workers saved my life that night.

When I read this note it brought tears to my eyes. It's humbling to realize that something as simple as a peanut butter sandwich can have the power to save a young boy's life.

I'm so grateful to friends like you who allowed our outreach team to be there for Dennis the night he needed us.

No child should be forced to eat out of the trash. And with your support, they won't..

I wish you could climb on board one of our outreach vans and join us in our work. After riding around with us for a couple of hours, you would see very clearly how your support helps these frightened, desperate children.

Night after night, we hit the streets. We see the kids gathering on the street corner even before our van rolls to a stop.

They come out of boarded-up buildings and dark alleys. They look so young – some of them are barely teenagers. They tear open the lunch bags we give them and gulp down their sandwiches in quick, hungry bites.

Food is just one of the things we offer these boys and girls. We provide basic first aid for children who need it and counseling for those who want it. A big part of what we do is just listen.

I wish I could tell you that after talking with us, these kids climb on board our van and come back to our shelter at Covenant House. I really wish I could – but that's not usually how it works out.

More often, we'll talk with a child for many nights, getting to know him and showing him he can trust us. Sometimes it takes weeks before a teenager will do anything more than take a lunch bag, mumble "thank you" and disappear back into the darkness.

The key is that they know we're out there.
That we're here to help them.

Right now we're seeing many more children trying to survive on the streets. That's typical during the summer. Kids who are getting beaten up at home often strike out on their own once the weather gets warm.

They think living on the streets is easier at this time of year. You might think so too. But it's not.

You see, the places these kids find to stay are filthy. They might wind up sleeping in a sweltering hot tenement that has garbage rotting in the hallways and is infested with cockroaches and rats.

And that's not the worst of it. As the mercury goes up, people's tempers get shorter. It's easy to tell the kids are being knocked around – either by their pimps or johns or drug dealers. Even in the shadows under the street lamps, you can see the ones who have a split lip or bruises on their face.

That's why I really need your help. <u>We must get these boys and girls to safety as quickly as possible.</u>

If we can reach a child within the first two weeks after he's run away from home, the chance of getting him off the streets is pretty good.

But after that, it gets a lot harder. By the time the kids have been on their own for two weeks, they've fallen prey to the human vermin who prowl the streets. They've been hurt and abused in sickening ways. Any shred of innocence they had has been ripped away.

After what they've been through, it's not surprising they don't trust anyone. You can see it in their eyes... in the way they act tough to prevent anyone from hurting them again.

Because you are one of our most compassionate friends, I'm hoping and praying you will help us save one more needy child today.

Our outreach workers talk to hundreds of kids every week. ***It costs $45 to keep one of our vans on the street for one hour.*** That covers the cost of bag lunches, gas for the van and other necessities.

If you can help us stay on the road – for even just an hour or two – you'll let us reach out to dozens of

boys and girls like Dennis who are sleeping in dirty alleys and eating out of dumpsters.

With you by our side, we can give them a fresh start and a more promising future.

And it all starts by giving a hungry boy or girl food to eat – something like a peanut butter sandwich.

How do I know these simple things make a difference? Easy – people like Dennis tell me so. Here's the rest of the letter he sent me...

> *I'm married now, with a boy of my own. The other day I was fixing my son a peanut butter and jelly sandwich for lunch, and I thought of Covenant House. I thought about that sandwich you offered me – with no strings attached – and all the help I got in the shelter.*
>
> *Then I looked at my little boy and thought about all the things in life I would have missed if I never got off the streets.*
>
> *For the rest of my life, every time I make my son a sandwich, I will think of Covenant House and say a little prayer of thanks to God.*
>
> *I just wanted you to know that. God bless you.*

Please help us. There are so many other homeless, abandoned kids like Dennis who are struggling to survive on our city's cruelest streets.

They need our help. And we need yours.

Your generous contribution will keep our outreach teams rolling. It will let us offer a homeless teenager a bag lunch, guidance and a chance to get off the streets – as well as the love and compassion every child deserves.

The American Family

I passionately believe the breakdown of the family unit is the single deepest ethical and moral challenge of our generation. And whether we respond to it will depend on the resolve and willingness of all of us to commit ourselves to the care and protection of family life. The time for repairing endangered families and rescuing their children is not after they have fallen apart!

The question then is ... how? How can each of us make a difference in protecting the American family? And how can we begin to make that difference now?

Because the survival of the family is so very important to our futures, we have prepared this special Family Survival Guide. This Guide features the best things we've learned working with hundreds of thousands of young people, as well as good, time-tested values that we never let ourselves forget. Please share these pages with a parent you know who may need help. Thank you so much!

Sister Tricia Cruise

Family
Survival
Guide

**Reflections on
Raising Children Today**

Who runs away?

What comes to mind when you think of children who run away from home? Teenagers off on an adventure, looking for a good time? Young people who can return home when their adventure is over?

Or maybe you think of the young people who make trouble at school? Who don't want to listen to their parents or anybody? Who just want to do what they want to do?

Or perhaps you think of young people with lots of problems and parents who don't care?

Really, there's no one way to describe young people who are homeless. They are males and females; from rich families and poor families. They may be your daughter or sister, nephew or friend.

We do know one thing – there are a lot of them — more than one million are runaways and 500,000 are homeless a year!

The odds are high that you will know someone who will run away before they turn 18 – one in every 12 young people do.

Running from ... not running to

Most young people don't run away seeking fame, fortune and adventure. They're running from what they fell are unbearable or unsolvable situations. They're running away because they just don't know what else to do – but they know they have to do something.

While only about six percent of the kids who leave home stay on the streets or keep returning to the streets, that's still tens of thousands of young people every year!

Many kids who return home run again and again and keep running, because usually without help nothing changes. But things CAN change. Help is available – at Covenant House.

A Special Message to Young People

Before you run away...

Though sometimes it is necessary and even healthy to leave a dangerous or abusive situation at home, think carefully about your reasons before acting. Imagine leaving a hurtful family only to be constantly abused and in danger on the street.

Consider ...

– Is it dangerous stay at home?

– Is there someone at home who will listen if you can find the right way to let them know there's a problem?

– Do you know anyone else you can talk to – someone who can help you figure out a way?

– If you leave, where will you go on the first night? What about the next nights?

- Before you leave, call the Covenant House Nineline (1-800-999-9999.)

A Special Message to Parents

Values ... Teaching in Today's World

Communicating your values has never been more important than it is today. And the good news is, it all begins and ends with you.

When all is said and done, parents have far more influence over instilling values in their children than any other factor.

Here are some simple, and very important things we should all remember about values, and passing them along:

- Kids get their sense of what's right and wrong from people they love and respect. No one has more influence over teaching values than you do. Your input can make all the difference!

- When it comes to teaching values ... actions always speak louder than words. Children need to see the values lived out by you. Respect for life, respect for other people, honesty, integrity ... kids get those by watching you.

- Families are still the best vehicle for raising children. A loving, nurturing family unit, of whatever form, creates the kind of environment kids need to learn what's right from wrong ... and how to love themselves, too.

- Always strive to teach your kids to love and respect themselves as children of God. A healthy love and respect for themselves is incredibly important for any kid. It's also the first essential step in helping a kid also learn a love and respect for those around him.

You've got a tough job...

None of us were ever taught to be parents. So we can't help but disappoint ourselves sometimes. How often have you heard yourself using the very same words you hated hearing from your own parents?

And when our kids become teenagers, it gets even harder. They seem to reject everything we've taught them. As far as they're concerned, we know nothing. Our values and beliefs are constantly challenged. Every word we utter is seen as interference. Emotions run high.

But we're more important to our teens than ever. As they try out the values of their peers, who are more influential than ever, we counter the pull of drugs and alcohol. These entangle children every day and can ruin their lives.

The stakes are high...

Teenagers who don't get what they need at home look elsewhere. Some run away from home. Many more consider other ways of running from pressure ...

a once bright and happy son escapes to drugs ... a vivacious daughter starts drinking. Think about these facts:

- Each year, one million students drop out of high school or are chronically truant.
- Four out of 10 teenage girls will become pregnant before age 20.
- One in four teens develops a drinking problem during his teen years; about 10,000 will die in alcohol-related accidents this year.
- Each year, 5,000 to 6,000 teens die in suicide-related deaths, and the number is growing, one every 90 minutes. For every death, at least 100 other young people attempt suicide.

The Turbulent Teens...

Teens face pressures that adults don't take seriously. Their bodies are changing – they have to adjust to the new person they see in the mirror. They feel different. They become interested in sex.

Self-doubt is constant. They feel pressure to conform and fear ridicule if they don't.

These changes can be bewildering, frightening, and even depressing.

Teens can have remarkable insights. But they also surprise us with their lack of good judgment.

How Well Do You Know Your Kids?

You may say, "My teenager wouldn't do that," Most don't. But even if yours wouldn't, think about the following questions:

- Where is your child right now?
- What are your teens deepest fears?
- Who is your son's or daughter's best friend?
- Do your teen's friends feel welcome in your home?

Remember, a strong relationship with your children is the best way for you to guide them and to prevent them from becoming a tragic statistic.

Getting Along with Your Teen...

Here are some ideas and techniques you can try to improve your relationship with your teen. If they don't work at first, keep trying. They take practice.

- Make time for your teen. Find an activity you enjoy doing together and pursue it. If your invitations are declined, keep asking.

- Listen, really listen. Because parents have so much to do and so little time, we often try to listen while cleaning, washing dishes or fixing the car. Put your chores aside so your teen knows you're really paying attention.

- Take the long view. Don't treat minor mishaps as major catastrophes. Choose important issues. Don't make your home a battleground.

- Tolerate differences. View your teenager as an individual distinct from you. This doesn't mean you can't state your opinion if you disagree.

- Respect your teenager's privacy. But if a behavior is worrying you, speak up.

- Let your teens sort things out themselves. Never say you know how your teen feels. They believe their feelings (so new and personal) are unique. They'll learn otherwise – without your help. And never imply that their feelings don't matter or will change. Because teens live in the present, it doesn't matter that they'll soon feel differently.

- Don't judge. State facts or opinions when you praise or criticize. Stating facts like "Your poem made me smile," or "This report card is all C's and D's" leaves it up to your teen to draw the appropriate conclusions. Teens are sensitive about being judged – positively as well as negatively.

- Be generous with praise. Praise your child's efforts, not just accomplishments. And don't comment on the person. "You're a great artist" is hard to live up to. "I loved that drawing" is a fact and comes from your heart.

- Set reasonable limits. Teens need them. Your rules should be consistently applied – and rooted in your deepest beliefs and values.
- Teach your teen to make sensible decisions and choices by encouraging independence and letting your teenager make mistakes. Don't step in unless you have to.

Signs That Your Child Needs Outside Help...

- Suicidal talk of any kind. A suicidal teen may also give away valued possessions, make a will, talk about death or dying or say his family would be better off without him.

- Recent changes in sleeping or eating habits, thinking patterns, personality, friendships, study habits, activities. A sudden unexplained end to a long depression often precedes a suicide attempt. Major weight loss can be a sign of bulimia or anorexia – dangerous problems.

- Drug or alcohol use. You might notice: irrational or irresponsible behavior, lying, secretiveness, severe mood swings, a sudden increase in accidents. A teen with a problem may have dilated pupils or wear sunglasses indoors, or complain about not sleeping or feeling well. Valuables may disappear. You may find drug paraphernalia or alcohol containers around the house.

- A recent change in friends who you feel may be involved with drugs or alcohol may indicate that your child is involved or be a sign that your child is having other problems.

- Law-breaking behavior, even if the police and courts aren't involved. You might notice new possessions and money not accounted for.

- Poor self-image. Doubts are normal. But persistently low self-esteem is a problem.

- Serious depression. Listlessness, loneliness, withdrawal, difficulty making friends.

- Rebelliousness to the point of total, continual defiance.

- Problems at school, including class cutting, absenteeism, a sudden drop in grades.

- Fears or anxieties that interfere with everyday activities.

- Problems between family members that aren't solved by listening and discussing. In fact, family changes such as death, divorce or remarriage are times when teens often need some outside help.

When to get help for yourself...

- Things aren't going well with your family but you can't figure out why.

- You totally disagree with positions your spouse has taken on issues concerning your teen and you can't find a compromise.
- You have trouble holding a job.
- You are abusing drugs or alcohol.
- You get violent with your teenager and can't control yourself.
- Your spouse gets violent with you or your child.

What to do if your teen runs away...

Most children who run away return within 48 hours. Those who stay away can find themselves in many dangerous situations. So do everything you can to bring your child home.

- Keep a notebook recording steps you've taken and the dates.
- Check in with: neighbors, relatives, and your teen's friends, teachers, employer or co-workers
- Contact local hangouts and hospitals.
- Call the police. Have an officer come to your house and take a report and pick up recent photos, dental records and fingerprints if available. Get the officer's name, badge number and phone number; the police report number, and the name of the officer who will follow up.
- Call the Covenant House Nineline for support and to check for messages. Leave a message

with us. Also, check with any local runaway hotlines.

- Contact runaway shelters locally and in nearby states.

- Make posters with photos of your teen, listing: height, weight, hair and eye color complexion, physical characteristics (such as scars, birthmarks, braces or pierced ears) circumstances of disappearance, your phone number and police contacts. Distribute these to truck stops, youth-orientated businesses, hospitals, law enforcement agencies.

- Be prepared for the first conversation with your teen. Whether in person or by phone, show concern, not anger. Say, "I love you."

- Prepare to quickly begin resolving the problems which cause your child to leave home. When your child returns home, emotions are likely to run high. Someone outside your family can help you deal with these emotions. You may find that planned time for your teen is a temporary residence or shelter is necessary while you are resolving problems. So get outside help from a trained counselor.

Need expert help or support?

Call our NINELINE counselors
at
1-800-999-9999.

We'll put you in touch with
people who can help you right
in your hometown.

1-800-999-9999

COVENANT HOUSE
Sister Patricia A. Cruise, S.C., President
346 West 17th Street
New York, NY 10011-5002
(212) 727-4000
Fax: (212) 727-4992
E-Mail: SisterTricia@CovenantHouse.org
Home page: http://www.covenanthouse.org

COVENANT HOUSE NEW YORK
Bruce J. Henry, Executive Director
460 West 41st Street
New York, NY 10036-6801
Fax: (212) 947-2478
E-Mail: info@covenanthouseny.org
http:// www.covenanthouseny.org

COVENANT HOUSE ALASKA
Deirdre Phayer, Executive Director
609 F Street
Anchorage, AK 99501-3533
Mailing Address:
P.O. Box 104640
Anchorage, Alaska 99510-4640
(907) 272-1255
Fax: (907) 272-9548
E-mail: dphayer@covhouse.alaska.com
http://www.covenanthouseak.org

COVENANT HOUSE CALIFORNIA
George R. Lozano, Executive Director
(323) 461-3131
E-Mail: info@covca.org
http://www.covdove.org

Los Angeles
Covenant House California
1325 N. Western Avenue
Hollywood, CA 90027-5615
(323) 461-3131
Fax: (323) 461-6491

Oakland/East Bay Program
Covenant House California
2781 Telegraph Ave.
Oakland, CA 94612-1733
(510) 625-7800
Fax: (510) 625-7811

COVENANT HOUSE FLORIDA
James M. Gress, Executive Director
(954) 561-5559
E-Mail: jgress@covenanthouse.org
http://www.covenanthousefl.org

Fort Lauderdale
Covenant House Florida
733 Breakers Avenue
Fort Lauderdale, FL 33304-4116
(954) 561-5559
Fax: (954) 565-6551

Orlando
Covenant House Florida
5931 East Colonial Drive
Orlando, FL 32807-3452
(407) 482-0404
Fax: (407) 482-0657

COVENANT HOUSE GEORGIA
Maxine Shoulders-Brandon, Executive Director
2488 Lakewood Ave., S.W.
Atlanta, GA 30315
(404) 589-0163
Fax: (404) 832-1282
E-Mail: MShouldersBrandon@CovenantHouse.org

COVENANT HOUSE MICHIGAN
Sam Joseph, Executive Director
2959 Martin Luther King, Jr. Boulevard
Detroit, MI 48208-2475
(313) 463-2000
Fax: (313) 463-2001
E-Mail: SJoseph@covenanthouse.org
http://www.covenanthousemi.org

COVENANT HOUSE MISSOURI
11 South Newstead Avenue
St. Louis, MO 63108-2213
(314) 533-2241
Fax: (314) 533-2215
E-Mail: cfagan@covenanthousemo.org
http://www.covenanthousemo.org

COVENANT HOUSE NEW JERSEY
James White, Executive Director
(973) 621-8705
E-Mail: jwhite@covenanthouse.org
http://www.covenanthousenj.org

Newark
Covenant House New Jersey
330 Washington Street
Newark, NJ 07102-2630
(973) 621-6680

Atlantic City
Covenant House New Jersey
3529 Pacific Avenue
Atlantic City, NJ 08401
(609) 348-4070
Fax: (609) 348-1122

COVENANT HOUSE NEW ORLEANS
Stacy Horn Koch, Executive Director
611 North Rampart Street
New Orleans, LA 70112-3505
(504) 584-1108
Fax: (504) 584-1171
E-Mail: shornkoch@covenanthouse.org
http://www.covenanthouseno.org

COVENANT HOUSE PENNSYLVANIA
Jerome Kilbane, Executive Director
417 Callowhill Street
Philadelphia, PA 19123-4018
(215) 923-8370
E-Mail: jkilbane@covenanthousepa.org

COVENANT HOUSE TEXAS
Rhonda Robinson, Executive Director
1111 Lovett Boulevard
Houston, TX 77006-3823
(713) 523-2231
Fax: (713) 523-6904
E-Mail: sfife@covenanthouse.org
http://www.covenanthousetx.org

COVENANT HOUSE TORONTO
Ruth daCosta, Executive Director
20 Gerrard Street East
Toronto, Canada M5B 2P3
(416) 598-4898
Fax: (416) 204-7030
E-Mail: general@covenanthouse.on.ca.
http://www.covenanthouse.ca

COVENANT HOUSE VANCOUVER
Sandy (Charles) Cooke, Executive Director
575 Drake Street
Vancouver, British Columbia
Canada V6B 4K8
(604) 685-5437
Fax: (604) 685-5324
E-Mail: info@covenanthousebc.org
http://www.covenanthousebc.org

COVENANT HOUSE WASHINGTON
Judith Dobbins, Executive Director
2001 Mississippi Avenue, SE
Washington, DC 20020
(202) 610-9600
Fax: (202) 610-9610
http://www.covenanthousedc.org

COVENANT HOUSE LATIN AMERICA
Casa Alianza
346 West 17th Street
New York, NY 10011-5002
(212) 727-4097
E-Mail: jharnett@covenanthouse.org

Just a reminder …
Many companies match their employees' charitable donations. Please check with your company or your spouse's company. It could mean extra help for our kids. Thank you!

Your Part of the Covenant

Covenant House depends almost entirely on gifts from friends like you to help almost 80,000 homeless and runaway children every year. We provide food, clothing, shelter, medical attention, educational and vocational training and counseling to young people with no place to go for help. Please help if you can.

YES! I want to help the kids at Covenant House.
Here is my gift of   ❑ $10   ❑ $20   ❑ $25   ❑ Other

Name _____

Address _____

City _____ State _____ Zip _____

Please make your check payable to Covenant House.
Your gift is tax deductible.

❑ Please send me your financial information.
❑ Please send me _____ copies of *God, Thank You for the Morning.*

Many people like to charge their gift. If you would like to, please fill out the information below:
I prefer to charge my:
❑ American Express ❑ Master Card ❑ Discover ❑ Visa

Account # _____

Amount_____ Exp. Date_____

Signature _____

Mail to: COVENANT HOUSE
JAF Box 2973
New York, NY 10016-2973
Or call 1-800-388-3888 to charge your gift. Thank you!
